Be Active

by Mari Schuh

T0084499

PEBBLE
a capstone imprint

Pebble Explore is published by Pebble, an imprint of Capstone
1710 Roe Crest Drive
North Mankato, Minnesota 56003
www.capstonepub.com

**Library of Congress Cataloging-in-Publication Data is available on
the Library of Congress website.**
ISBN: 978-1-9771-2384-8 (library binding)
ISBN: 978-1-9771-2684-9 (paperback)
ISBN: 978-1-9771-2421-0 (eBook PDF)

Summary: There are so many ways to be active. Play tag. Go on a
bike ride. Take a hike! Learn about the importance of being active in
this book.

Image Credits
iStockphoto: FatCamera, 13, 18, 21; Shutterstock: AlohaHawaii, 24, B
Wright, 16, BlueSkyImage, 27, fizkes, 23, Golden Pixels LLC, 12, Iakov
Filimonov, 29, Jose Gil, 17, michaeljung, 9, Monkey Business Images,
5, People Image Studio, 22, Photographee.eu, 11, photonova, Cover,
design element, pixinoo, Cover, Rawpixel.com, 20, Rob Marmion,
8, Sergey Novikov, spread 14-15, Spotmatik Ltd, 25, TinnaPong, 7,
Zurijeta, 19

Editorial Credits
Editor: Christianne Jones; Designer: Sarah Bennett; Media Researcher:
Morgan Walters; Production Specialist: Laura Manthe

All internet sites appearing in back matter were available and
accurate when this book was sent to press.

Table of Contents

Bold words are in the glossary.

Move It

Have you moved your body today? Did you play at recess? Maybe you walked to school. Maybe you played T-ball.

Some kids enjoy soccer. Other kids like to skate. There are so many ways to be active! What is your favorite way to get moving?

Healthy and Strong

Why is it good to move your body? It keeps you healthy and strong! It builds strong bones. When you are active, your lungs work harder. They take in more oxygen. This makes your lungs stronger. Exercise makes your heart strong too.

Being active makes your muscles strong and **flexible**. Your **balance** and **posture** get better when you are active. Exercise can also help you be a healthy weight.

Staying active feels good! Exercise gives you more energy. You might feel very happy. You might worry less.

People who are active often sleep better. But try not to exercise right before you go to bed. It might be hard to go to sleep.

Being active helps you in many ways. It can help you **focus**. You might have more energy to learn. Exercise also helps you feel better about yourself. It gives people **confidence**.

Get Ready

Before you exercise or play, make sure you are ready. Take some time to warm up your body. Do some stretches. Take some deep breaths.

You might go to the doctor for a checkup. You will learn about your health.

Make sure to be safe when you exercise. Always listen to your body. Exercise should not hurt. Stop if you are hurt. Tell an adult you know.

Kids should be active about one
hour a day. Good news! You can do it
in small parts. Maybe you play kickball
at recess. Then you swim after school.
It all adds up to one hour.

Set **goals** to move every day. Make plans to play with friends. Sign up for new sports. Limit your time on phones and computers. That gives you more time to play.

What you wear when you play is important. The right shoes keep you from getting hurt. Dress shoes are not good for running. Old shoes can hurt your feet. Be sure to wear a helmet when you ride your bike.

If you play outside, think about the weather. A baseball hat will keep the sun out of your eyes. Wear sunscreen to protect your skin. Is it hot? You might want to wear shorts. Is it windy? Be sure to bring a coat.

Playing Sports

Sports are lots of fun. They are also a great way to be active. When you play sports, you move your muscles. Your heart pumps. Your lungs work hard. Sports help keep your body fit.

What sport do you want to play? If you like to run, try basketball. Or you might like soccer. Do you want to play inside? Try **karate** or gymnastics.

Sports help you learn many skills. You learn to follow rules. Sports teach you how to play fair. You also learn teamwork. Be a good friend when you play. Cheer for others. Be nice to all the kids on the team.

Don't want to join a team? You can play sports in other ways. Run with a classmate. Play catch with your mom. Ask your friends to swim with you. Shoot hoops at home. Mix it up!

Be prepared when you play sports. Make sure you have the equipment you need. Wear your team uniform. Bring your water bottle. Get ready to play!

Take good care of your body. Warm up before you are active. You might do jumping jacks. Do a few arm circles.

After you play, be sure to stretch gently. Stretch your whole body. Breathe slowly and deeply. Be sure to drink extra water.

Moving in Many Ways

Don't enjoy sports? No problem! There are many ways to be active. You can exercise at home. Count how many sit-ups you can do. Then do a few push-ups. Try **yoga**.

Don't want to miss your favorite TV show? Exercise while you watch TV. See how many jumping jacks you can do. Dance to music. Turn up the volume and have fun!

You don't have to go far to exercise outside. You can be active in your backyard. Play in the leaves. Build a snowman. Play catch with a friend.

Get moving with your family. Ride your bikes. Do a **scavenger hunt**. Go for a hike. Walk your dog. Make up your own race. You can hop, skip, and jump. You can jog or sprint. Think of different ways to move your body!

It's important to be active all year. Is it snowing outside? Put on a coat and bundle up. It's time to go sledding!

In bad weather, be safe and exercise inside. Be active at home or find an indoor play space. Climb and play. Play tug-of-war. Don't let bad weather keep you from being active.

You can stay active by planning your day. Have an adult help you. Choose how you want to spend your free time. Be mindful of how much time you spend on electronics. Make sure you have time to exercise.

Take care of your body by staying active. Exercise keeps your whole body healthy. It gives you energy and keeps you fit. And it's lots of fun!

Glossary

balance (BAL-uhnss)—to keep steady and not fall over

confidence (KON-fuh-duhns)—a feeling or belief that you can do well

flexible (FLEK-suh-buhl)—able to bend or move easily

focus (FOH-kuss)—to keep all your attention

goal (GOHL)—something that you aim for or work toward

karate (kah-RAH-tee)—a martial art using controlled kicks and punches

posture (POSS-chur)—the way in which your body is positioned when you are sitting or standing

scavenger hunt (SKAV-uhn-jur HUHNT)—a game in which people look for hidden items

yoga (YOH-guh)—exercises and ways of breathing that keep the mind and body healthy

Read More

Black, Vanessa. *Exercise*. Minneapolis: Jump!, Inc., 2017.

Rustad, Martha, E.H. *I Stay Active*. North Mankato, MN: Capstone Press, 2017.

Stratton, Connor. *We Exercise*. Lake Elmo, MN: Focus Readers, 2020.

Internet Sites

Kids Health: Be a Fit Kid
https://kidshealth.org/en/kids/fit-kid.html#catfit

MyPlate Kids' Place: Be a Fit Kid
https://choosemyplate-prod.azureedge.net/sites/default/files/audiences/Tipsheet2_BeAFitKid.pdf

Workout Time!
https://pbskids.org/arthur/health/fitness/workout-time.html

Index